**W9-AHB-895**

# The U.S. Constitution

## Government by the People

We the People of the United States, in Order to form a more perfect Union, establish Justice, insure domestic Tranquility, provide for the common defence, promote the general Welfare, and secure the Blessings of Liberty to ourselves and our Posterity, do ordain and establish this Constitution for the United States of America.

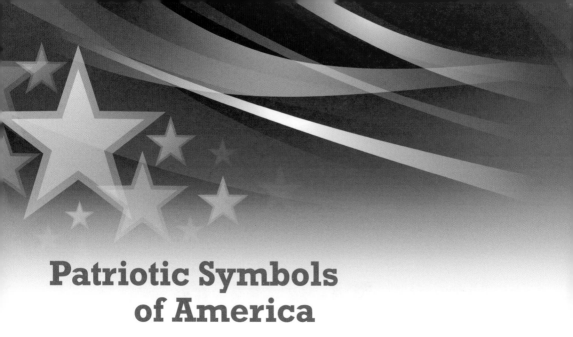

# Patriotic Symbols
# of America

# The U.S. Constitution

## Government by the People

Hal Marcovitz

**Mason Crest**
Philadelphia

**Mason Crest**
450 Parkway Drive, Suite D
Broomall, PA 19008
www.masoncrest.com

© 2015 by Mason Crest, an imprint of National Highlights, Inc.

Printed and bound in the United States of America.

CPSIA Compliance Information: Batch #PSA2014. For further information, contact Mason Crest at 1-866-MCP-Book.

Publisher's note: all quotations in this book come from original sources, and contain the spelling and grammatical inconsistencies of the original text.

First printing
1 3 5 7 9 8 6 4 2

Library of Congress Cataloging-in-Publication Data

on file at the Library of Congress

ISBN 978-1-4222-3133-3 (hc)
ISBN 978-1-4222-8756-9 (ebook)

Patriotic Symbols of America series ISBN: 978-1-4222-3117-3

# Contents

---

**KEY ICONS TO LOOK FOR:**

**Text-dependent questions:** These questions send the reader back to the text for more careful attention to the evidence presented there.

**Words to understand:** These words with their easy-to-understand definitions will increase the reader's understanding of the text, while building vocabulary skills.

**Series glossary of key terms:** This back-of-the book glossary contains terminology used throughout this series. Words found here increase the reader's ability to read and comprehend higher-level books and articles in this field.

**Research projects:** Readers are pointed toward areas of further inquiry connected to each chapter. Suggestions are provided for projects that encourage deeper research and analysis.

**Sidebars:** This boxed material within the main text allows readers to build knowledge, gain insights, explore possibilities, and broaden their perspectives by weaving together additional information to provide realistic and holistic perspectives.

# Patriotic Symbols and American History

**S**ymbols are not merely ornaments to admire—they also tell us stories. If you look at one of them closely, you may want to find out why it was made and what it truly means. If you ask people who live in the society in which the symbol exists, you will learn some things. But by studying the people who created that symbol and the reasons why they made it, you will understand the deepest meanings of that symbol.

The United States owes its identity to great events in history, and the most remarkable American Symbols are rooted in these events. The struggle for independence from Great Britain gave America the Declaration of Independence, the Liberty Bell, the American flag, and other images of freedom. The War of 1812 gave the young country a song dedicated to the flag, "The Star-Spangled Banner," which became our national anthem. Nature gave the country its national animal, the bald eagle. These symbols established the identity of the new nation, and set it apart from the nations of the Old World.

To be emotionally moving, a symbol must strike people with a sense of power and unity. But it often takes a long time for a new symbol to be accepted by all the people, especially if there are older symbols that have gradually lost popularity. For example, the image of Uncle Sam has replaced Brother Jonathan, an earlier representation of the national will, while the Statue of Liberty has replaced Columbia, a woman who represented liberty to Americans in the early 19th century. Since then, Uncle Sam and the Statue of Liberty have endured and have become cherished icons of America.

Of all the symbols, the Statue of Liberty has perhaps the most curious story, for unlike other symbols, Americans did not create her. She was created by the French, who then gave her to America. Hence, she represented not what Americans thought of their country but rather what the French thought of America. It was many years before Americans decided to accept this French goddess of Liberty as a symbol for the United States and its special role among the nations: to spread freedom and enlighten the world.

This series of books is valuable because it presents the story of each of America's great symbols in a freshly written way and will contribute to the students' knowledge and awareness of them. It it to be hoped that this information will awaken an abiding interest in American history, as well as in the meanings of American symbols.

— Barry Moreno,
librarian and historian
Ellis Island/Statue of Liberty National Monument

 ## Words to Understand

**Congress**—the lawmaking branch of the federal government.

**credit**—advancement of money and goods to a customer, who promises to repay with interest.

**inflation**—an economic condition in which the value of money lessens.

**legislature**—the governing body of a state composed of representatives elected by the people.

**militia**—Fighting force of volunteers, usually organized by a state or local government.

Daniel Shays, a Massachusetts farmer, address-
es a crowd of supporters on the steps of the
courthouse in Northampton, Massachusetts.
Shays's 1786 rebellion was a sign that people
were unhappy with the federal government
that had been created in the colonies after
the American Revolution. Soon, a new system
of government, based on a document called
the U.S. Constitution, would be established.

# Shays's Rebellion

When Daniel Shays returned to his farm in
Massachusetts after the American War for
Independence, he expected to enjoy the freedoms he
fought hard to win as a captain in the Continental Army.

But throughout the 13 states, things were getting off
to a rocky start. After seven years of war, the treasuries
of the state governments were empty. They had been
drained by the costs of outfitting the Continental Army
and waging war against the army of King George III.

The state *legislatures* were forced to levy high taxes.
What's more, the new nation was troubled by *inflation*.
This is an economic condition that results in high prices
for food, tools, and other goods. Farmers like Daniel
Shays found it difficult to raise enough crops to feed
their families and pay their taxes and debts. Before the

war, farmers could often pay their debts by trading livestock or crops grown in their fields. Now, the store owners who sold them seed on *credit* and the bankers who loaned them money demanded to be repaid in gold or silver.

In the years following the Revolutionary War, falling into debt was a serious offense, punishable by imprisonment. By August of 1786, many farmers found themselves so much in debt that they could no longer hold onto their farms. Their creditors would go to court and win the approval of judges to seize the farms and sell them at auction. Many farmers had to stand by helplessly while auctioneers sold their land to pay off their debts.

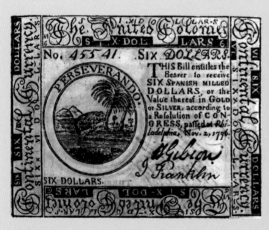

This is the front and back of a six dollar bill from the time of the American Revolution. After the colonies won their independence, they were faced with a money shortage and high taxes to pay for the war with England.

On August 29, 1786, a mob of angry farmers stormed the courthouse in Northampton, Massachusetts, to prevent the court from sitting that day. The mob leaders reasoned that if the judges could not preside over cases in their courtrooms, they could not order farms to be taken from poor, debt-ridden farmers. The mob was led by Daniel Shays. The attack on the courthouse in Northampton was the beginning of what became known as the "Shays's Rebellion."

Word of the rebellion spread quickly throughout Massachusetts as well as the other states. The leaders of the government were horrified that the self-rule they had won during the Revolution was being questioned so soon after the war.

At first, Massachusetts Governor James Bowdoin looked to the federal government to help put down Shays's Rebellion. But the *Congress* could do little. Since 1781, the federal government of the United States had operated under laws known as the Articles of Confederation. This was a weak set of rules that gave the states immense authority to govern themselves. The articles provided Congress power to make laws, but no authority to make the states comply with them. What's more, under the articles the federal government could not raise taxes. This meant it could not pay for an army to defend the states. And so, Massachusetts would receive no help from the federal government in putting down Shays's Rebellion.

Meanwhile, Shays struck again. In September 1786, he and 600 followers closed the courts in Springfield, Massachusetts.

Bowdoin found that his state also lacked the money to pay an army to put down the rebellion. So the governor turned to wealthy landowners in the state, who provided money for the *militia*. Bowdoin sent 4,400 militia members to Springfield, and Shays was soon chased away.

Shays and his men returned to Springfield on January 25, 1787. This time, Shays led a mob of 2,000 members. They intended to attack and capture an arsenal, where they could find guns and ammunition.

Again, Bowdoin dispatched the militia. The mob was dispersed and Shays was captured.

Massachusetts was not the only place in America where poor farmers rebelled against taxes and debt. In Maryland, angry farmers attacked the Charles County Courthouse, successfully closing down the courts. In Camden, South Carolina, a mob closed down the courthouse and chased the judges home. In Virginia, a mob burned down the King William County Courthouse.

Congress decided it was time to act. The Articles of Confederation had not given the Congress and federal government enough power to enforce the law. Also, the inability of the federal government to respond to Shays's Rebellion showed that, in times of crisis, the government was powerless. And so, a "Constitutional Convention"

## VITAL FIGURE: Daniel Shays

Daniel Shays led an armed rebellion against the courts of Massachusetts that called attention to the need for a strong national government and a set of strong yet fair laws to guide people's lives.

Shays was born in 1747 in Hopkinton, Massachusetts. During the War for Independence, he served as a captain in the Continental Army and fought at the battles of Bunker Hill, Stony Point, and Saratoga.

Following the war, he returned to his farm in Pelham, a town in western Massachusetts. Soon Shays found himself upset about high taxes and debt. The rebellion he led lasted just five months. It was eventually put down by the Massachusetts militia under orders from Governor James Bowdoin.

Shays and some 200 followers were arrested and tried for treason. Shays was convicted and condemned to hang, but he had become an enormously popular hero among the poor farmers of western Massachusetts. He was granted a pardon in 1788 by John Hancock, who had replaced Bowdoin as governor.

Shays died in 1825. He remains a hero in western Massachusetts, with streets and highways named in his honor.

was called in Philadelphia for the purpose of framing a new set of laws that would guide the nation into the future and make the federal government an important force in the lives of the people of America.

### Text-Dependent Question
What was the first form of government that was created to enable the 13 American colonies, later states, to work together?

### Research Project
Shortages of money were a problem throughout all of the British colonies of North America. Visit this website maintained by the Federal Reserve Bank of Philadelphia, http://www.philadelphiafed.org/education/teachers/resources/money-in-colonial-times, to find out more about the problems involving coinage and paper money in 18th century America.

# Words to Understand

**constitution**—a document containing the laws of a state or nation.

**delegate**—a representative to a meeting.

**draft**—an early form of a written document.

**House of Representatives**—the lower legislative body of Congress, composed of representatives whose numbers are determined by each state's population.

**impasse**—the inability of two or more parties to agree on a solution.

**judiciary**—the branch of government consisting of the courts.

**jury**—a body of impartial citizens who decide guilt and innocence in a courtroom.

**president**—the chief executive of a government whose authority is provided by vote of the people.

**Senate**—the upper legislative body of Congress, composed of two members from each state.

**veto**—the right to cancel an act of the government, usually exercised by a governor or president.

George Washington presides over the Constitutional Convention, which was held in Philadelphia in 1787. Washington had led the Continental Army to victory during the American Revolution. Though he retired for a few years after the war ended in 1783, he was asked to lead the committee tasked with creating a new form of government for the United States.

# A More Perfect Union

Across America, leaders of the state governments wondered about the 55 *delegates* called to Philadelphia for the Constitutional Convention in the summer of 1787. People were very loyal to their home states in the years after the War for Independence. Their ancestors had followed religious leaders to America and helped establish the colonies in the New World that eventually became the 13 original states. Patrick Henry, a statesman from Virginia whose speeches helped convince his countrymen to fight for independence from England, was suspicious of the convention. Rhode Island refused to send delegates to the convention and, later, became the last of the 13 states to ratify the

*Constitution*. Even George Washington had his doubts. "I almost despair of seeing a favorable issue to the proceedings of the convention, and do therefore repent having any agency in the business," he said.

Nevertheless, Washington agreed to preside over the convention as it opened in the Pennsylvania Assembly's State House on the morning of May 14, 1787. "Let us raise a standard to which the wise and honest can repair," Washington told the delegates. "The event is in the hands of God."

The delegates got down to business on May 29 and started by reviewing the "Virginia Plan," a *draft* of the Constitution written mostly by James Madison. According to Madison's draft, Congress would be divided into two chambers—a *House of Representatives* and a *Senate*. Congress would be charged with writing the nation's laws while a separate executive branch of government was given authority to carry out the laws. Finally, a third branch of government, the *judiciary*, was given the power to interpret the nation's laws, ensuring that they would be applied equally to all citizens.

After some debate, the delegates agreed to adopt the Virginia Plan's model for the three branches of government. However, the delegates continued to fight over the details. For example, since the end of the Revolution the larger states had complained about the "one state-one vote" makeup of the Congress. It meant that a small state, such as Rhode Island, had just as much power in

## VITAL FIGURE: James Madison

James Madison was 36 years old when the Constitutional Convention convened in Philadelphia. He wrote most of the draft that would eventually be adopted as the blueprint for the nation's laws, earning him the nickname "Father of the Constitution."

Madison served first in the Virginia Assembly, where he wrote the constitution for his state. His main achievement as author of the Virginia Constitution was the inclusion of a guarantee of religious freedom.

Following adoption of the U.S. Constitution, Madison served in Congress, where he helped establish the departments of State, War and Treasury. In 1801, President Thomas Jefferson named him secretary of state. Madison's negotiations with France led to the Louisiana Purchase. Thirteen future states would be formed out of the western territory America obtained from France for about $15 million.

Madison was elected president in 1808 and led his country through the War of 1812. During his presidency, the White House became the center of Washington style and society, thanks to the influence of his wife, Dolley Madison.

The Madisons retired from public life in 1817 and lived quietly at Montpelier, their estate in Virginia. James Madison died in 1836.

Congress as a large state like Virginia. Delegates from the large states argued against one state-one vote at the Constitutional Convention while delegates representing the small states vigorously called for the current system to remain intact.

Finally, delegate Roger Sherman of Connecticut offered a compromise that broke the *impasse*. He suggested membership in the House of Representatives be

Roger Sherman, a delegate from Connecticut, had served on the Continental Congress from 1774 to 1784, and helped draft both the Declaration of Independence and the Articles of Confederation. In 1787, he helped to craft the Constitution by suggesting a compromise on the way states would be represented in the federal government.

based on the population of the states, with the larger states sending more representatives than the smaller states. Membership in the Senate would be equal, he said, with each state guaranteed two members. While the Connecticut Compromise seemed to satisfy no one, few of the delegates found a reason to vote it down, and it was accepted.

Next, the delegates defined the role of Congress, giving the House and Senate power to "lay and collect taxes, duties, imposts and excises" and to write laws it deemed "necessary and proper." That was far more power than the Articles of Confederation had granted.

The judiciary was placed in the hands of the "Supreme Court," composed of nine judges who would have the power to decide all "cases arising under the laws passed by the general legislature." After some debate, it was decided the Supreme Court would hear cases without a *jury*.

And the delegates gave the Congress and Supreme Court vast powers so that the authority over the states would never be questioned. The Constitution would be the "supreme Law of the Land."

There was much debate over the *president's* powers, as well as how the president would be chosen.

The Virginia Plan suggested the president be selected by Congress. Pennsylvania delegates James Wilson and Gouverneur Morris proposed the president be elected directly by the people. Finally, a compromise was reached: Each state would name members to an "Electoral College." The electors would be selected in a manner to be decided by each state legislature. The Electoral College would then meet to select the president.

Following the Constitutional Convention, each state legislature decided to choose its electors through a popular election, giving the people a direct voice in the selection of the president. Today, when a presidential candidate wins the popular vote in a state, he typically receives all of that state's votes in the Electoral College.

Next, the delegates had to decide how long the president would serve. There were proposals to name the president for life. After debate, however, the delegates agreed to limit presidential terms to four years.

Throughout the summer, there were a thousand details to be worked out, prompting a thousand debates.

**Make Connections**

James Madison's notes and papers from the Constitutional Convention were considered the only accurate record of the meeting's proceedings. In 1837, Congress appropriated $30,000 to buy the papers from Madison's estate.

For example, the delegates decided that a president could be removed from office, that the president had to have been born in America, and that the president would have *veto* power but that Congress could override the veto.

As the summer wore on, the temperatures eased and so did the tempers. Benjamin Franklin helped unite the delegates when he announced his support for the Constitution. He said, "I consent, Sir, to this Constitution because I expect no better, and because I am not sure that it is not the best."

By early September, the delegates appointed a five-man "Committee of Style and Arrangement" to draft the Constitution—to place in writing the agreements that had been reached during the debates in the State House. Madison was named to the committee. Others selected for the panel were Gouverneur Morris and Alexander Hamilton as well as delegates William Samuel Johnson of Connecticut and Rufus King of Massachusetts.

There was no question that it was largely Madison's document—the Constitution adopted many of the principles of the Virginia Plan. But Morris wrote the preamble—the introduction to the Constitution. Morris's preamble set the tone for the document to follow, serving

## VITAL FIGURE: Gouverneur Morris

He was a lawyer and expert in finance, but Gouverneur Morris's greatest skill was in the use of language. His talent for crafting words was so well known to the other delegates at the Constitutional Convention that they asked him to help put the Constitution in its final form. It was Morris who wrote the preamble to the Constitution.

He was born and educated in New York, where he established a law practice and helped write his state's constitution. He joined the Continental Congress in 1778, but was defeated for reelection a year later. Soon, he was back in Congress, where he helped plan the nation's system of using dollars for currency. After the Constitutional Convention, he served as a diplomat in France.

After his service in France, Morris returned to New York, where he won election to the United States Senate. He died in 1816.

notice to the citizens of the United States that they would live under a nation of laws written, enforced, and interpreted by representatives of the people.

But before the final document was ready, some of the delegates would ask for a change. They wanted the document to clearly state all the rights that would be given to all American under the new constitution.

### Text-Dependent Questions

What was the "Virginia Plan?" Why did the representatives of smaller states feel that it did not protect their interests?

### Research Project

An important responsibility of the U.S. Supreme Court is to determine whether laws are in accordance with the Constitution. Choose one of the nine current justices, and write a report about that person. Use your local library or the Internet to learn about their life. Supplement your report with pictures of the justice.

 **Words to Understand**

**amendment**—a change to the Constitution, approved by three-quarters of the states.

**libel**—published words that purposely lie about an individual to make him or her look bad.

**ratification**—approval.

**redress**—making right what is wrong.

Andrew Hamilton, a colonial lawyer, argues for his client, John Peter Zenger, during Zenger's 1735 trial for libel. Zenger was eventually acquitted of the charges. The Zenger trial established the American tradition of freedom of the press—one of many freedoms that the Constitution guarantees.

# The Bill of Rights

The American tradition of freedom of the press goes back to a court case decided more than 50 years before the Constitutional Convention.

In 1731, William Cosby was appointed governor of New York by King George II of England. He arrived from London in 1732, aiming to rule the colony with an iron fist. He demanded fees collected from New York merchants by the former governor; he fired judges who would not do what he wanted and appointed his own friends to their positions; he rigged elections; he forced landowners to pay high taxes when they sold their land; and he even seized land for himself.

The public learned of Cosby's crimes through the work of John Peter Zenger, publisher of the *New York Weekly Journal*, a newspaper in colonial New York. For months, Zenger's newspaper kept up a constant barrage of attacks on Cosby.

On December 3, 1733, the newspaper accused the governor of having opponents kicked out of town council meetings and of letting French warships spy on the colony from New York Harbor. Every copy of the newspaper sold, and Zenger was forced to print extra copies.

Cosby reacted angrily to the *Journal*'s stories. He had Zenger arrested for "Scandalous, Virulent and Seditious Reflections Upon the Government." When Zenger arrived in court to defend himself against the charges, he found the trial rigged against him—his own lawyer had been replaced by one of the governor's friends.

However, Zenger's friends had gone to Pennsylvania and hired a lawyer themselves. He was Andrew Hamilton, a member of the Pennsylvania Assembly and a believer in the rights of individuals. When the trial opened, Hamilton strode to the front of the courtroom and announced he would be taking over Zenger's defense. As the trial proceeded, the spectators were stunned by Hamilton's arguments. He admitted the Zenger had published the newspapers, but said that it was his right, and indeed the right of all, to publish the information, so long as it was true.

The prosecutor suggested that since Hamilton had admitted Zenger published the attacks on the governor, the jury had no choice but to convict the defendant. Hamilton argued that just publishing the stories was not a crime, saying, "The words themselves must be *libelous*—that is, false, malicious and seditious—or else we are not guilty."

Hamilton told the jury that the case "may in its consequence affect every free man that lives under a British government on the main of America. It is the best cause. It is the cause of liberty."

The jury returned a verdict of not guilty. It was the first time in colonial America that an individual's freedoms had triumphed over the tyranny of a ruler. Forty-one years later, the colonies declared their independence from England, contending that King George III refused to recognize the rights of individuals.

"Every man who prefers freedom to a life of slavery will bless and honor you," Andrew Hamilton told the

## VITAL FIGURE: Andrew Hamilton

Andrew Hamilton died 46 years before the meeting of the Constitutional Convention. Yet his fierce defense of the freedom of speech and the right to a fair trial laid the groundwork for the Bill of Rights.

Hamilton was born in Scotland in 1676. He immigrated to America in 1700, settled in Philadelphia and took up the practice of law. In 1717, he joined the Provincial Assembly of Pennsylvania and later became its speaker. In this position, he led the drive to establish the State House in Philadelphia. Hamilton picked the location for the building and designed the structure himself. Later, the State House would serve not only as the location of the Constitutional Convention, but also as the place where the Continental Congress met to debate the Declaration of Independence. In 1824, the State House was renamed Independence Hall.

jurors after the Zenger trial. "The laws of nature and of our country have given us a right—the liberty—both of exposing and opposing arbitrary power by speaking and writing truth."

As the Constitutional Convention came to an end in Philadelphia in September 1787, many delegates wondered why they had failed to include a "Bill of Rights" in the document they had labored over all that summer. One of those delegates was George Mason of Virginia, who said he could not sign the Constitution until it included a Bill of Rights.

Years before, Mason had drafted a "Declaration of Rights" for Virginia when it was still a colony. Mason's declaration was a set of laws Virginia adopted to protect the rights and property of its citizens. The Declaration of Rights had served as an inspiration to Thomas Jefferson as he wrote the Declaration of Independence.

Still, the Constitution was signed by the delegates and ratified by the 13 state legislatures. It was now the supreme law of the United States. But its framers had included a way for Congress and the states to make changes. On October 2, 1789, George Washington, who had been elected the first president of the United States, submitted to Congress a list of 12 *amendments* to the U.S. Constitution. The amendments had been written by James Madison, who became convinced that rights such as free speech, a fair trial, and the right to bear arms should carry the weight of federal law.

George Mason, a delegate to the Constitutional Convention from Virginia, wanted a Bill of Rights to be added to the document. Mason said that until the document included a Bill of Rights, he would "sooner chop off his right hand than put it to the Constitution [to sign]."

Congress eliminated the first two amendments—they dealt with pay for members of Congress as well as size of congressional districts. But the other 10 amendments were sent on to the states for *ratification*, and they became the Bill of Rights.

The First Amendment addressed the issues raised in the Zenger trial, as well as other rights that the king had denied to the colonists. "Congress shall make no law respecting the establishment of religion, or prohibiting the free exercise thereof; or abridging the freedom of speech or of the press, or the right of the people to peaceably assemble, and to petition the government for a *redress* of grievances," the amendment says.

In other words, the government could not tell any American how to worship, or what they could and could not say in public or print in their newspapers. People had a right to gather in public to protest against the

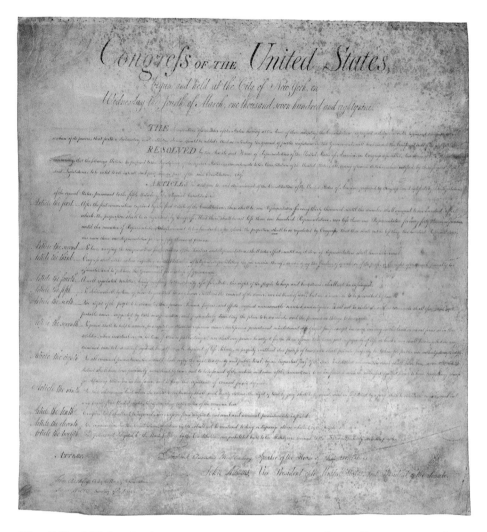

The Bill of Rights is the name given to a group of ten Constitutional amendments that define and protect the rights of Americans.

government, and to take their complaints directly to their government leaders.

The Second Amendment gave people the right to own guns. The Third Amendment prohibited the government from making people provide homes for soldiers—a common practice during colonial times.

The Fourth Amendment provided security in the home. It prevented agents of the government from barging down people's doors to search their homes without "probable cause," meaning the government had to suspect a crime had been committed in the home.

The Fifth, Sixth, and Seventh Amendments protected the rights of people accused of crimes and guaranteed fair, public, and speedy trials—all of which Governor Cosby had attempted to deny Zenger in 1735. The Eighth Amendment spoke against "cruel and unusual punishment," meaning the penalty had to fit the crime.

The Ninth Amendment stated that people possessed rights that may not be addressed in the Constitution and that the government must respect those rights. Finally, the Tenth Amendment addressed the rights of the states. It said any power the Constitution did not reserve for the federal government would become the responsibility of the states.

By December 1791, the state legislatures approved the amendments, and the Bill of Rights was made a part of the Constitution.

**Text-Dependent Questions**

How many amendments does the Bill of Rights include? How many of those amendments deal with the rights of individuals?

**Research Project**

Over the past 40 years, the intent of the Second Amendment has been hotly disputed, due in part to its wording. Some people believe the amendment was meant to empower state militias, not permit all private citizens to own firearms. Read the amendment, then go online and examine both sides of the issue. Then write a report about how you interpret the amendment, explaining and justifying your decision.

 **Words to Understand**

**Federalists**—name for people who supported ratification of the U.S. Constitution in the late 1780s. Alexander Hamilton, James Madison, and John Jay were key members, and wrote many essays and letters explaining how the new Constitution would benefit Americans.

**inauguration**—a formal ceremony at which a person is placed in an official position, such as president of the United States.

On July 4, 2003, the National Constitution Center opened in Philadelphia, not far from Independence Hall. The center features numerous exhibits, including *Freedom Rising*, an inspirational 17-minute-long film that runs throughout each day.

# Facts About the Constitution

**O**nce the preamble was completed, the U.S. Constitution was turned over to Jacob Shallus for "engrossing." This meant Shallus had to write out, by hand, the words the delegates had argued over and voted on during the summer.

Shallus was an expert penman who was employed as the assistant clerk of the Pennsylvania Assembly to engross the assembly's documents. It was Shallus who wrote out the words "We the People" in large, bold letters, leaving little doubt in a reader's mind exactly for whom the document was written.

Shallus was paid $30 to engross the Constitution.

Fifty-five delegates debated the Constitution during the summer of 1757. Nineteen other delegates had been appointed by their colonies to attend the Constitutional Convention but never showed up. They either declined to attend or shirked their responsibilities.

Rhode Island refused to send delegates, fearing that its lucrative shipping trade would be harmed with a change in government. New Hampshire's delegates did not arrive until July 23. Two out of the three New York delegates left early, leaving only Alexander Hamilton in attendance from that state. Without the other two delegates in attendance, Hamilton didn't feel he had the authority to cast the ballot for his state, so New York exercised no vote throughout much of the summer.

Although the delegates concerned themselves with writing laws, not all of them were lawyers. Thirty-four of the 55 delegates practiced law; the others were soldiers, farmers, teachers, clergymen, physicians, bankers, and merchants. Benjamin Franklin, at age 81, was the oldest delegate. Jonathan Dayton of New Jersey, age 26, was the youngest.

John Adams and Thomas Jefferson, the two men most responsible for the Declaration of Independence, did not participate in the writing of the Constitution. At the time of the Constitutional Convention, Adams was serving as American ambassador to Great Britain while Jefferson held that position in France. Later, Jefferson called for the addition of the Bill of Rights.

The Constitutional Convention ended on September 17, 1787. On that day, George Washington wrote in his journal: "The business being closed, the members adjourned to the City Tavern, dined together and took cordial leave of each other after which I returned to my lodgings and retired to meditate on the momentous work which had been executed."

Disputes over the Constitution led to the establishment of political parties in America. People who supported the Constitution called themselves *Federalists* while opponents became known as the Anti-Federalists. Anti-Federalists opposed the Constitution because they believed it would create a central government that would become too powerful and dominated by wealthy people, and that the federal government would take power away from the states.

Eventually, all 13 states did vote for ratification. The first to ratify was Delaware, followed by Pennsylvania, New Jersey, Georgia, Connecticut, Massachusetts, Maryland, South Carolina, New Hampshire, Virginia, New York, North Carolina and Rhode Island. The Constitution became effective when the ninth state, New Hampshire, ratified the document on June 21, 1788. On September 13, 1788, Congress instructed the states to send representatives to the Electoral

**Make Connections**

As the delegates toasted the completion of the Constitution in the City Tavern in Philadelphia, printers John Dunlap and David Claypoole worked into the night to publish the first copies of the six-page document; it was ready for delivery to the state legislatures the next morning.

The preamble to the Constitution reads:

**We the People of the United States, in Order to form a more perfect Union, establish Justice, insure domestic Tranquility, provide for the common defence, promote the general Welfare, and secure the Blessings of Liberty to ourselves and our Posterity, do ordain and establish this Constitution for the United States of America.**

College on the first Wednesday in February 1789, for the purpose of selecting a president. On that day, George Washington was elected president with 69 electoral votes. Twelve electors did not cast ballots. Two electors each from Virginia and Maryland declined to vote, and none of the eight electoral votes allocated to New York were cast because the state legislature could not agree on how to select the electors.

Government under the old Articles of Confederation ended on March 3, 1789. The next day, Congress met for the first time under the rules established by the Constitution. And on April 30, 1789, George Washington took office as the nation's first president.

The *inauguration* was in New York City, which served as the capital of the United States at the time. The oath was administered to Washington on a balcony overlooking Broad and Wall streets by Robert R. Livingston, a New York state official, who asked Washington to swear that he would "preserve, protect and defend the Constitution of the United States."

Thirty-eight of the delegates to the 1787 convention in Philadelphia signed the Constitution, yet the document contains 39 signatures. George Read, a delegate from Delaware, signed for himself as well as John Dickinson, who had gone home because he became sick. The National Constitution Center has an exhibit that includes statues of all the signers.

Washington answered, "I swear, so help me God!"

Livingston then turned to the crowd below and announced: "Long live George Washington, president of the United States!"

### Text-Dependent Question
Why didn't John Adams and Thomas Jefferson participate in writing the U.S. Constitution?

### Research Project
With a group of friends, write a skit re-enacting the drafting of the U.S. Constitution. Make sure to explain in the dialogue why this document was drafted, and discuss important points that the delegates to the Constitutional Convention argued over in 1787. When your skit is completed, perform it for the class with your friends.

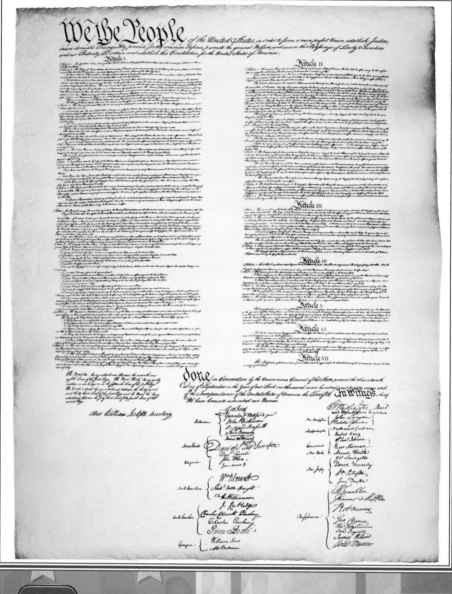

# Words to Understand

**Prohibition**—a period in American history when the sale, manufacture, and transportation of alcohol was illegal. Prohibition went into effect in 1920 after ratification of the Eighteenth Amendment. The Twenty-first Amendment, ratified in 1933, ended Prohibition.

A copy of the U.S. Constitution. The 1787 Constitutional Convention was held in the Pennsylvania State House, which 11 years earlier had housed the Continental Congress during the debate over the Declaration of Independence. In 1824, the building was renamed Independence Hall.

# "The Best Government"

The U.S. Constitution is a part of every American's life.

Around Christmas time, why are there no nativity scenes displayed in the lobby of the county courthouse? Because the Constitution says there must be a separation of church and state. Why are hate groups such as the Ku Klux Klan permitted to hold rallies in public squares and parade on city streets? Because the Constitution guarantees every American the right to free speech. Why are people permitted to own handguns and other deadly weapons? Because the Constitution says Americans have the right to bear arms. Why is the criminal told about his rights at the time of his arrest? Because the Constitution says he is entitled to a fair trial.

> **Make Connections**
>
> In 1887, during a celebration of the 100th anniversary of the U.S. Constitution, British Prime Minister William E. Gladstone called it "the most wonderful work ever struck off at a given time by the brain and purpose of man."

As a protector of the rights of the individual, the Constitution does its job. But the Constitution is not perfect. It has to be fixed from time to time.

The document approved by the delegates in 1787 permitted slavery. In fact, it gave the slave-holding states extra representation in the House of Representatives. According to Article 1, Section 2 of the Constitution, when calculating the number of representatives that a state would send to the U.S. House, "three fifths of all other persons" would be added to the number of free persons residing in that state. Therefore, according to the Constitution, a slave was worth three-fifths of a free person. The slave was regarded as property by his owner and received none of the rights guaranteed by the Constitution. Following the Civil War, the Thirteenth Amendment to the Constitution outlawed slavery. Other amendments gave former slaves the rights of citizenship.

Women had no right to vote in America until the Nineteenth Amendment was passed in 1920, thanks to many years of struggle by right-to-vote activists. But an amendment that would guarantee women other rights— such as equal pay and fair treatment in the workplace—

failed to pass the state legislatures by its 1982 deadline. Although some groups hope to resurrect the so-called "Equal Rights Amendment," as of 2014 it remains in limbo.

After the turn of the century, the *Prohibition* movement gained strength in America. Prohibitionists wanted alcoholic beverages to be outlawed. The movement was led by such groups as the Women's Christian Temperance Union. They got their wish in 1919 when the Eighteenth Amendment was passed.

The first African slaves in North America are delivered to the English colony at Jamestown, 1619. Although the Declaration of Independence states that "all men are created equal," a paragraph blaming King George III of England for allowing slavery in America was taken out of the final draft because Thomas Jefferson did not want to offend southern leaders. The Founding Fathers made no provisions to end slavery in the U.S. Constitution. It would not be until 1865, when the Thirteenth Amendment was passed, that slavery would be forever abolished in the United States.

California residents cast their ballots during the 2012 presidential election. American women did not gain the right to vote until the Nineteenth Amendment was passed in 1920.

Adoption of the amendment led to a widespread crime wave in America. Gangsters found ways to import, manufacture, and sell liquor to otherwise law-abiding citizens. Federal authorities found it virtually impossible to enforce the law. In 1933, the Twenty-First Amendment was adopted, repealing prohibition.

During the 1960s, America found itself fighting a war in Vietnam. Soon, it became necessary to draft young men to fight the war. Men as young as 18 were called to duty in the jungles of Southeast Asia. It was a war that few people understood or supported, and soon many of the young men who were drafted wanted to know why they were old enough to fight for their country, yet not old enough to vote. In most states the legal voting age was 21. In 1971, the 26th Amendment to the Constitution was adopted, setting the voting age at 18.

Did James Madison and the other framers of the Constitution know the document they produced in Philadelphia would have to change as America changed? There is no question they did—that is why they included Article Five, which specified how the Constitution could be amended.

Following the ratification of the original document, the Bill of Rights as well as another 17 amendments would be added to the U.S. Constitution—evidence that the document produced during the summer of 1787 was a work in progress, essentially a blueprint for the laws of the United States and rights of American citizens.

Near the end of his life, Madison wrote, "That which is the least imperfect is therefore the best government." More than 225 years after it was ratified, many Americans still believe that the U.S. Constitution remains the best governmental framework that has ever been produced.

**Text-Dependent Questions**
What Amendment gave women the right to vote? When was it ratified?

**Research Project**
The Thirteenth Amendment to the Constitution, ratified in 1865, formally abolished slavery in the United States. Find out more about the history of this amendment at this online Library of Congress exhibit—
http://www.loc.gov/rr/program/bib/ourdocs/13thamendment.html.

# Chronology

**1781** Continental Congress adopts the Articles of Confederation.

**1783** American War for Independence ends.

**1786** Mob led by Daniel Shays closes down the courthouse in Northampton, Massachusetts, on August 29.

**1787** Shays' Rebellion put down by Massachusetts militia on January 25; Constitutional Convention convenes in Philadelphia on May 14, ending on September 17.

**1788** Constitution becomes law when the ninth state, New Hampshire, votes to ratify on June 21.

**1789** Electoral College selects George Washington the first president of the United States on February 17; he takes the oath of office April 30; Bill of Rights proposed for addition to the Constitution on September 25.

**1791** The Bill of Rights is ratified on December 15.

**1804** Following the controversial election of 1800 that initially resulted in a tie, the Twelfth Amendment, concerning presidential election procedures, is passed.

**1868** The Fourteenth Amendment, establishing equal rights for all U.S. citizens, is passed.

**1913** The system of income tax is established by the Sixteenth Amendment. Rules regarding term limits for senators are imposed by the Seventeenth Amendment.

**1920** The Nineteenth Amendment grants women the right to vote.

**1971** The Twenty-Sixth Amendment lowers the legal voting age from 21 to 18.

**1992** The Twenty-Seventh Amendment, which prohibits midterm Congressional pay raises, is ratified.

**2003** The National Constitution Center, a museum devoted to explaining the importance of the U.S. Constitution, opens in Philadelphia.

**2010** The U.S. Supreme Court includes three female justices for the first time with the appointment of Elena Kagan.

# Series Glossary

**capstone**—a stone used at the top of a wall or other structure.

**cornerstone**—the first stone placed at a spot where two walls meet, usually considered the starting point of construction.

**dome**—an element of architecture that resembles the hollow upper half of a sphere.

**edifice**—a large building with an imposing appearance.

**facade**—the decorative front of a building.

**foundation**—the stone and mortar base built below ground that supports a building, bridge, monument, or other structure.

**hallowed**—holy, consecrated, sacred, or revered.

**keystone**—the architectural piece at the crown of a vault or arch which marks its apex, locking the other pieces into position.

**memorial**—something designed to help people remember a person or event in history.

**obelisk**—a shaft of stone that tapers at the peak.

**pantheon**—a public building containing monuments to a nation's heroes.

**pedestal**—the base or support on which a statue, obelisk, or column is mounted.

**portico**—a roof supported by columns, usually extending out from a building.

**rotunda**—a large and high circular hall or room in a building, usually surmounted by a dome.

**standard**—a flag or banner that is adopted as an emblem or symbol by a nation.

**symbol**—an item that represents or stands for something else.

# Further Reading

Alarcon, Robert. *The Constitution and the Bill of Rights*. Huntington Beach, Calif.: Teacher Created Materials, 2008.

Cheney, Lynne. *We the People: The Story of Our Constitution*. New York: Simon and Schuster, 2012.

Landau, Elaine. *The Declaration of Independence*. New York: Children's Press, 2008.

Marcovitz, Hal. *The Declaration of Independence*. Philadelphia: Mason Crest Publishers, 2014.

Middlekauff, Robert. *The Glorious Cause: The American Revolution, 1763-1789*. New York: Oxford University Press, 2007.

Mulhall, Jill K. *The Declaration of Independence*. Huntington Beach, Calif.: Teacher Created Materials, 2008.

Nash, Gary B. *The Liberty Bell*. New Haven: Yale University Press, 2011.

Pederson, Charles. *The U.S. Constitution and Bill of Rights*. Minneapolis: Abdo, 2010.

Sands, Robert W., and Alexander B. Bartlett. *Independence Hall and the Liberty Bell*. Mount Pleasant, S.C.: Arcadia Publishing, 2012.

Staton, Hilarie. *Independence Hall*. New York: Chelsea Clubhouse, 2009.

Strum, Richard. *Causes of the American Revolution*. Stockton, NJ: OTTN Publishing, 2006.

Taylor-Butler, Christine. *The Constitution of the United States*. New York: Children's Press, 2008.

Wood, Alexander. *Visit Independence Hall*. New York: Gareth Stevens, 2012.

# Internet Resources

**http://www.loc.gov/law/help/second-amendment.php**

This page from the Library of Congress provides a history of how the U.S. Supreme Court has interpreted the Second Amendment, as it relates to private gun ownership, over the years.

**http://www.constitutioncenter.org**

The National Constitution Center is a museum devoted to the U.S. Constitution and its legacy of freedom. The Center, which is located in Philadelphia, features numerous interactive exhibits, films, and rare artifacts related to the Constitution from the 1780s to the present day.

**http://www.archives.gov/federal-register/electoral-college/about.html**

The official website of the Electoral College provides information about this body and its role in U.S. presidential elections.

**http://www.ourdocuments.gov**

The National Archives' online exhibit "Our Documents" provides information about 100 milestone documents in American history, including the U.S. Constitution. The site includes images of each document, transcripts, and links to informative articles.

**http://www.nps.gov/inde**

National Park Service website of Independence National Historical Park in Philadelphia, which includes Independence Hall, where the Constitution was written. The site includes a wealth of information for teachers and students.

# Index

# Index

# Picture Credits

# Contributors

**BARRY MORENO** has been librarian and historian at the Ellis Island Immigration Museum and the Statue of Liberty National Monument since 1988. *The Statue of Liberty Encyclopedia* (2000), *The Encyclopedia of Ellis Island* (2004), *Ellis Island's Famous Immigrants* (2008), and *The Ellis Island Quiz Book* (2011). He also co-edited a scholarly study on world migration called *Leaving Home: Migration Yesterday and Today* (2011). His biography has been included in *Who's Who Among Hispanic Americans*, *The Directory of National Park Service Historians*, *Who's Who in America*, and *The Directory of American Scholars*. Mr. Moreno lives in New York City.

**HAL MARCOVITZ** has written more than 100 books for young readers. He lives in Chalfont, Pennsylvania, with his wife, Gail. They have two grown daughters, Ashley and Michelle.